FIND OUT ABOUT
ROCKS
AND MINERALS

With 23 projects
and more than
350 pictures

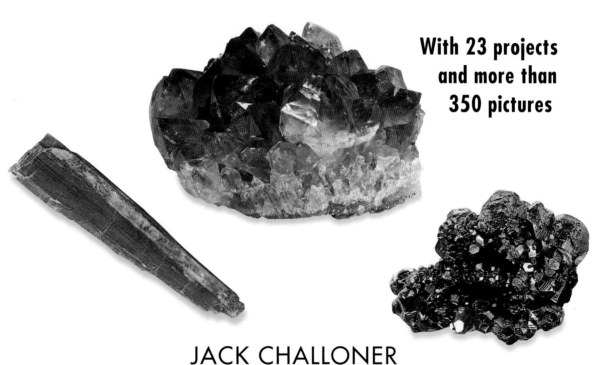

JACK CHALLONER

ARMADILLO

This edition is published by Armadillo, an imprint of Anness Publishing Ltd,
Blaby Road, Wigston, Leicestershire LE18 4SE; info@anness.com
www.annesspublishing.com

If you like the images in this book and would like to investigate using them
for publishing, promotions or advertising, please visit our website
www.practicalpictures.com for more information.

PICTURE CREDITS (b=bottom, t=top, m=middle, l=left, r=right)
Bridgeman Art Library: 58br, 59br. British Antarctic Survey: 34t. British Geological Survey: 25t, 35tl, 45bl,
48br. Thomas Chatham: 11br. Bruce Coleman Ltd/S. Bond: 19tr; /J. Cancalosi: 51bl; /J. Cowan: 39tl, 41br;
/D. Croucher: 19bl; /G. Cubitt: 38bl; /J. Foott: 19tl; /C. Fredriksson: 44b; /G. Harris: 41t; /J. Shaw: 58t.
De Beers: 10tl. Digital: 56br. E.T. Archive: 4t, 54t, 56bl, 58bl. Robert Harding: 40bl; /C. Bowman: 18tr;
/V. Englebert: 34bl&br. Frank Lane Picture Agency: 48bl, 54bl; /L. Batten: 41bl; /C. Carvalho:
24bl; Celtic Picture Agency: 5br; /S. McCutcheon: 24br, 27bl; /C. Mullen: 31bl; /M. Newman:
22t; /M.Niman: 18tl; /M.J. Thomas: 19mr; /R. Tidman: 23br; /T. Wharton: 45tr;
/W. Wisniewski 44t, 48tr. Microscopix Photolibrary: 11bl, 35tr, 45mr&br; /A. Syred: 35b.
Milepost 9½: 49tl. NASA: 23ml, 51br, 62t&mb, 63tl&ml. Natural History Museum: 48mt.
Natural History Photographic Agency/F. Mercay: 17bl. C. Oxlade: 31br. Papilio
Photographic: 9tl, 25b, 38br. Planet Earth Pictures: 17br, 29m, 63tr. Science Photo Library
/Crown Copyright, Health and Safety Laboratory: 57br; /F. Gohier: 63b; /A. & H.
Michler: 62mt; /P. Parviainen: 62b; /Photo Library International: 8t; /D. Weintraub: 16t.
Tony Stone: 29t&b, 31t, 39b, 49bl&br. Trip/J. Arnold: 40br; /International Colour
Stock: 39tr; /Phototake: 11t. University College London/A.R. Lord: 50. University
of Glasgow/Dr Gribble: 12br. Zefa Pictures: 54br.

Publisher: Joanna Lorenz	Stylist: Melanie Williams
Managing Editor: Sue Grabham	Designer: Caroline Grimshaw
Editor: Charlotte Hurdman	Picture Researcher: Caroline Brooke
Consultants: Dr Sue Bowler, Dr Bob Symes	Illustrations: Peter Bull Art Studio
Photographers: John Freeman, Don Last	Production Controller: Pirong Wang

PUBLISHER'S NOTE
Although the advice and information in this book are believed to be accurate and
true at the time of going to press, neither the authors nor the publisher can accept
any legal responsibility or liability for any errors or omissions that may have been
made nor for any inaccuracies nor for any loss, harm or injury that comes about
from following instructions or advice in this book.

Manufacturer: Anness Publishing Ltd, Blaby Road, Wigston,
Leicestershire LE18 4SE, England
For Product Tracking go to: www.annesspublishing.com/tracking
Batch: 0942-22415-1127

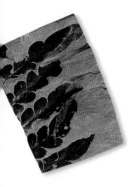

The publishers would like to thank...
Our models: Mitchell Collins, Ashley Cronin, Louise Gannon, Hamal Gohil,
Sarah Kenna, Catherine McAlpine, Griffiths Nipah, Goke Omolena, Ben Patrick,
Anastasia Pryer, Charlie Rawlings and Victoria Wallace.
Also: Mr and Mrs G R Evans.
And a special thank you to Gregory, Bottley and Lloyd for their efficient help
in supplying rock and mineral samples.

CONTENTS

ROCKS AND MINERALS

Rocks are the materials from which mountains, cliffs and the ground are made. Even sand, clay and soil are types of rock made from tiny particles. The processes that shape the rocks around us to form the landscape can take thousands or even millions of years. All rocks can be divided into three main groups – igneous, sedimentary and metamorphic rocks – according to the way in which they were formed. Just as rocks are the building blocks of the landscape, minerals are the building blocks of rocks. Minerals are naturally occurring substances found in the ground that are not part of an animal or a plant. About 3,500 different minerals have been identified. Some rocks contain only one mineral, but most are a mixture of two or more. Minerals include familiar substances, such as quartz and gold, and less familiar ones, such as kyanite and pyrite. Rock-forming minerals are constantly being recycled in a process called the rock cycle.

Gemstones
Minerals prized for their beauty and rarity are called gemstones. This ornament is made from the gemstone jade.

Minerals
All rocks are made up of one or more minerals. Minerals are natural, solid, non-living substances. Five different minerals are shown here: pyrite, kyanite, copper, opal and sulphur. Each one has definite characteristics, such as its shape and coloration, that distinguish it from all other minerals. Different combinations of minerals form many different types of rock.

Pyrite

Kyanite

Copper

Yellow sulphur crystals growing on kaolin

Opal in ironstone

The rock cycle

All rocks are constantly passing through a recycling process that has gone on for 3,500 million years. This is how igneous, metamorphic and sedimentary rocks form.

Granite

Sandstone

Rocks are worn into fragments and washed into the sea. They sink and compact into sedimentary rock, such as sandstone.

Molten rock rises to the surface where it cools to form igneous rocks, such as granite.

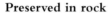

Gneiss

Heat from molten rock and pressure deep inside the Earth change surrounding sedimentary and igneous rocks. Metamorphic rocks, such as gneiss, form.

Preserved in rock

If rock forms around an animal when it dies, the outline of its body may be preserved as a fossil. Plants and even footprints can become fossils.

Inside a geode

Minerals usually grow in regular shapes called crystals. When mineral-rich water fills a crack or cavity in a rock, a geode may form. The beautiful crystal lining of a geode is revealed when it is split open.

Getting at rocks

We use rocks in many ways, but getting them out of the ground can be difficult. Explosives are often used to blast rocks out of cliff faces. Here limestone is being blasted out of a quarry.

LOOKING AT ROCKS

THE first thing you need to do when finding out about rocks and minerals is to become familiar with them. The best way to start is to look closely at a few rocks. You will find that they are not all the same. A magnifying glass will help you examine rocks closely. It gives an enlarged image of the rock, allowing you to see details that cannot be seen easily with the naked eye. Collect a wide variety of rock types so that you can compare them and learn to identify some of the various kinds. Testing the properties of minerals, such as hardness, can help to identify what sort of rock it is. Hardness is measured on a scale devised in 1822 by Friedrich Mohs. He made a list of ten common minerals, called Mohs' scale, which runs from 1 (the softest) to 10 (the hardest).

A closer look
Clean a rock with a stiff brush and water. Stand so that plenty of light shines on the rock and experiment to find the correct distance from the magnifying glass to the rock. Carefully sketch what you see.

Sieve

Chisel

Safety glasses

Rucksack

Hammer

Magnifying glass

Pencils

Penknife

Trowel

Camera

Notebook

Compass

Collecting bags

Map

Field guide

Water

Bucket

Helmet

Newspapers

Gloves

Rock collecting equipment
Wear protective clothing when you are out collecting rocks. Safety glasses, or goggles, will protect your eyes from any chips that might fly up when a rock is hit with a chisel. The helmet will protect your head from falling rocks. Search on the Web for good locations to visit, and take a map and compass to help you find them. Always take an adult with you when you are collecting rocks away from home.

Testing for hardness

1 Clean some rock samples with water using a nail brush. On Mohs' scale, a mineral is harder than any minerals that it scratches.

M A T E R I A L S

You will need: several rock samples, bowl of water, stiff brush, coin, glass jar, steel file, sandpaper.

2 A fingernail has a hardness of just over 2. Scratch each rock with a fingernail – if it scratches the rock, the minerals of which the rock is made have a hardness of 2 or less.

3 Put aside those rocks scratched by a fingernail. Use a coin to scratch the remaining rocks. A coin has a hardness of about 3, so any rocks it scratches contain minerals with a hardness of 3 or less.

The hardest natural mineral is diamond, with a hardness of 10. It will scratch all other minerals.

5 Put aside any rocks that will not scratch the glass. Try scratching the remainder with a steel file (hardness 7) and finally with a sheet of sandpaper (hardness 8).

4 Now try scratching the remaining rocks on a glass jar. If any scratch it they must be harder than glass, which has a hardness of between 5 and 6.

OUR ROCKY PLANET

EARTH is one of the planets that orbit the Sun. It is the most interesting planet for many reasons. For example, it is the only planet known to have liquid water and to have life. If you could cut Earth in half, you would see a central metal core, surrounded by a thick layer of molten rock called the mantle. Above the mantle is the Earth's surface – a thin, hard, rocky shell called the crust. There are two kinds of crust – oceanic crust (covered by the oceans) and continental crust (which forms the land). Some of the rocks in the continental crust are 3,500 million years old. The oceanic crust is newer, because it is constantly being formed as molten rock finds a way to the surface. Nowhere is the oceanic crust more than 200 million years old.

Earth from Space
From Space, you cannot see much of Earth's rocky crust – about two-thirds is covered with water. Beneath the cool blue appearance, lies a thin rocky crust and a fiery interior.

The Sun is a huge ball of extremely hot gas, almost entirely made of the elements hydrogen and helium.

Earth's place in Space
The planets are shown here in relative proportion to each other. The four inner planets are made of rock. The outer planets are mainly gas. Earth has the greatest variety of rocks, minerals and surface features of any planet.

Jupiter is a giant planet, big enough to fit all the other planets inside it.

Mercury is very small and rocky. It probably has a huge metal core.

Venus' structure may be similar to Earth's. Its thick clouds rain acid.

Earth is the largest and densest rocky planet. Its rocks are constantly changing.

Mars is a red desert of rocks, with large plains of volcanic lava.

The planets' relative distance from the Sun (below)

Mercury
Venus
Earth
Mars

Jupiter

Saturn

Hot rocks

Hot spots occur at points in the Earth's crust. This is where molten rock from the mantle comes close to the surface. The heat is used in geothermal power stations. Water is pumped underground, where it turns to steam. Steam-driven turbines generate electricity.

Crust (up to 40km/ 25 miles thick)

Mantle (about 2,900km/ 1,800 miles thick)

Outer core (about 2,000km/ 1,200 miles thick)

Inner core (about 1,300km/800 miles thick)

Thin crust

At its thickest point, the Earth's crust is only about 40 km (25 miles) thick. This is very thin compared to the size of the Earth. If a tomato was the Earth, its skin would be about as thick as the crust.

Saturn is another gas giant. Its impressive rings are made up of billions of rock particles. They have been observed since ancient times.

A slice through the Earth

The core of the Earth is made of metals. The central part of the core is solid, while the outer part is liquid. Surrounding the core is the mantle, and above that is the crust. Continental crust can be up to 40km (25 miles) thick beneath mountain ranges; oceanic crust is only about 6km (4 miles) thick.

Uranus' greeny-blue coloration is due to the ice and gas that surround its core.

Neptune is swept by the strongest winds in the Solar System.

Uranus

Neptune

WHAT ARE MINERALS?

Rocks are made up of minerals. For example, the igneous rock basalt, which makes up most of Earth's oceanic crust, is made of the minerals feldspar and pyroxene. Some minerals, such as sulphur and gold, are single elements (substances in which all the atoms are the same kind). Others are compounds of two or more elements. Feldspar is a compound of oxygen, silicon and aluminium with various other elements. The largest group of rock-forming minerals is the silicates, all of which include the elements silicon and oxygen. Quartz (the commonest mineral in the Earth's crust) is a silicate. The minerals inside a rock usually form small crystal grains that are locked together to form a hard solid.

The brilliant sparkle of a diamond is revealed when it is carefully cut and polished (top). A rough, uncut diamond (bottom) still has a gleaming lustre.

Just eight elements make up nearly all minerals in Earth's crust. Starting with the commonest first, they are: oxygen (1), silicon (2), aluminium (3), iron (4), calcium (5), sodium (6), potassium (7) and magnesium (8). All other elements make up (9).

Rock-forming minerals

Granite is one of the most common rocks found in the Earth's continental crust. It is made from three minerals – feldspar, mica and quartz. The minerals' crystals interlock as the molten rock cools. Quartz is grey and glassy, the feldspar is pale (often pink) and the mica is dark and silvery. Different granites can have different amounts of each mineral, which is why granite ranges in coloration from reddish-pink to grey.

Mica

Quartz

Granite

Feldspar

Pure gold

A few minerals occur as pure elements, not combined with other elements. Gold is a good example of a pure, or native, element. It is often found in veins with quartz. These formed when hot, watery liquid from volcanic rocks deposited the gold as it cooled in a crack in the rock.

Gold

Quartz

FACT BOX
- The word diamond comes from a Greek word *adamas*, which means "hardest metal".

- Rubies and sapphires are both rare forms of the mineral corundum, which is very hard. Small grains of corundum are called emery and are used on nailfiles.

- Ore minerals contain metals. About 60 types of pure metal are extracted from different ores.

Emerald in mass of mica schist

Real versus synthetic

Gemstones such as diamonds and emeralds are rare and expensive. Synthetic gemstones, like the cluster shown below, can be manufactured. This is done by subjecting the crystals of more common minerals to carefully controlled temperature and pressure.

Synthetic emerald

Vivid minerals

Under a microscope, a rock's tiny crystals appear large enough to study. Scientists can identify the minerals by special coloration produced by filters called polarizers.

Synthetic crystals can be made to grow in a particular size and shape, for a specific purpose. They are used in the electronics industry.

11

CRYSTAL SHAPES

I F you look closely at grains of salt, you will see that they are tiny cubes – each one is a minute crystal. Minerals nearly always form crystals, with characteristic shapes and coloration. The reason salt crystals are cubes has to do with tiny particles called ions, atoms and molecules. Molecules are groups of atoms, while ions are atoms (or groups of atoms) that have an electric charge. Each salt grain consists of billions of ions linked together in a cube-shaped pattern. There are seven different ways that atoms and molecules can join up to form a crystal. These are called crystal systems. A crystal grows as more particles are added to it. It does not always grow to reflect its crystal system, however, since there may be other crystals next to it. The way a crystal actually appears is called its habit.

Cubic: pyrite

Hexagonal: apatite

Orthorhombic: topaz

Triclinic: kyanite

Monoclinic: selenite

Trigonal: corundum

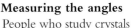

Tetragonal: vesuvianite

Crystals and glasses
The oranges in the bottom box are stacked in a disorderly way. Atoms that join like this do not produce crystals. Instead, they produce a material called a glass. In a crystal, atoms join together in an orderly way, like in the top box.

Crystal systems
A crystal can grow from molten minerals, or from minerals that are dissolved in liquids such as water. The geometric shape in which each mineral crystallizes is called its crystal system. There are seven main types, which are shown here. The mineral used to illustrate each crystal system is also named.

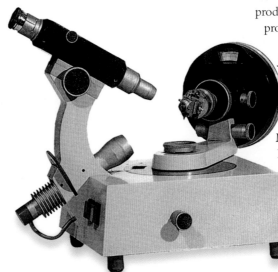

Measuring the angles
People who study crystals sometimes use a device called a goniometer. It measures the angles between the faces of a crystal. The angle helps to identify a mineral.

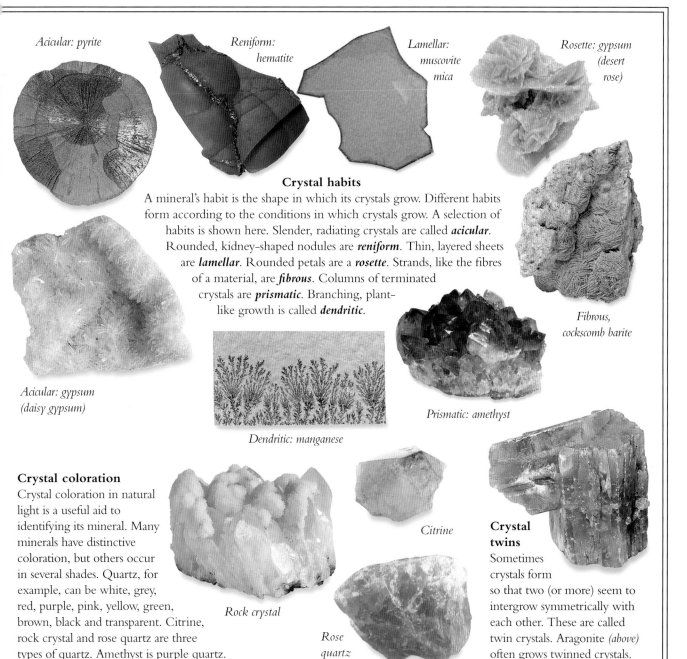

Acicular: pyrite

Reniform: hematite

Lamellar: muscovite mica

Rosette: gypsum (desert rose)

Crystal habits

A mineral's habit is the shape in which its crystals grow. Different habits form according to the conditions in which crystals grow. A selection of habits is shown here. Slender, radiating crystals are called *acicular*. Rounded, kidney-shaped nodules are *reniform*. Thin, layered sheets are *lamellar*. Rounded petals are a *rosette*. Strands, like the fibres of a material, are *fibrous*. Columns of terminated crystals are *prismatic*. Branching, plant-like growth is called *dendritic*.

Fibrous, cockscomb barite

Acicular: gypsum (daisy gypsum)

Dendritic: manganese

Prismatic: amethyst

Crystal coloration

Crystal coloration in natural light is a useful aid to identifying its mineral. Many minerals have distinctive coloration, but others occur in several shades. Quartz, for example, can be white, grey, red, purple, pink, yellow, green, brown, black and transparent. Citrine, rock crystal and rose quartz are three types of quartz. Amethyst is purple quartz.

Rock crystal

Citrine

Rose quartz

Crystal twins

Sometimes crystals form so that two (or more) seem to intergrow symmetrically with each other. These are called twin crystals. Aragonite *(above)* often grows twinned crystals.

MAKING CRYSTALS

Most solid substances – including metals – consist of crystals. To see how crystals form, think what happens when sugar is put into hot water. The sugar dissolves to form a solution. If you take the water away again, the sugar molecules are left behind and join up to reform into crystals. See this happen for yourself by trying the project below. Crystals can also form as a liquid cools to form a solid. In a liquid, the atoms or molecules are loosely joined together. They can move about, which is why a liquid flows. As the liquid solidifies, the molecules do not move around so much and begin to join together, usually to form a crystal. You can see this if you put a drop of water on to a mirror and leave it in a freezer overnight. Finally, make a simple goniometer and use it to measure the angles between the faces of some objects.

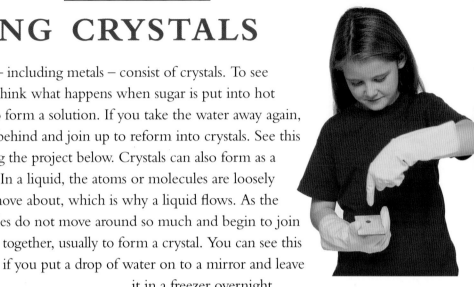

Ice crystals
A drop of water placed on to a dry mirror will spread out a little, then freeze solid in the freezer. Examine the crystals that form with a hand lens.

MATERIALS

You will need: water, measuring cup, pan, sugar, tablespoon, wooden spoon, glass jar.

Growing crystals

1 Ask an adult to heat half a litre (2 cups) of water in a pan until hot, but not boiling. Add as much sugar as will dissolve in the hot water.

2 Stir the solution well, then allow it to cool. Pour the cool solution into a glass jar and put it somewhere where it will not be disturbed.

3 After a few days or weeks, the sugar in the solution will gradually begin to form crystals. The longer you leave it, the larger your crystals will grow.

Making a goniometer

1 Draw carefully around the protractor on to a piece of cardboard using a dark felt-tip pen or pencil. Do not move the protractor.

2 With the protractor still in place, mark off 10° divisions around the edge. Remove the protractor to mark the divisions inside the semicircle.

3 Cut out the semicircle. Cut a thin rectangle of cardboard about 2cm (1in) longer than the semicircle's base. Cut one end into a point.

M A T E R I A L S

You will need: protractor, felt-tip pen or pencil, two pieces of cardboard, scissors, ruler, paper fastener.

A simple goniometer

5 Collect some objects with straight sides or faces. Rest the free end of the rectangle on the object. The other end will point to its angle on the scale. Real goniometers are more complex and more accurate, but they measure angles in a similar way to your home-made one and help to identify minerals.

4 Push the paper fastener through the pointer as shown and through the middle of the semicircle. Flatten out the fastener on the back.

MOUNTAINS OF FIRE

Ash in the air
A volcanic eruption produces tonnes of ash, as well as lava, often thrown high in the air. This is the 1980 eruption of Mount St Helens in the US.

THE molten rock in the Earth's mantle is called magma. At certain points on the Earth's surface, magma leaks out. These points are called volcanoes. Magma is called lava once it has reached the surface and lava solidifies to form volcanic rocks, such as pumice. The popular image of a volcano is a mountain that erupts violently, throwing ash and lava everywhere. Some volcanoes are like this, although they only erupt in this way once in a while. Fissures (or long cracks in the Earth's surface) also behave like volcanoes if lava flows from them. The cone of a large volcano is built up from solidified lava or ash that has erupted over many years. The magma is held in an underground chamber and escapes either continuously and slowly over a long time, or else rapidly in a violent eruption.

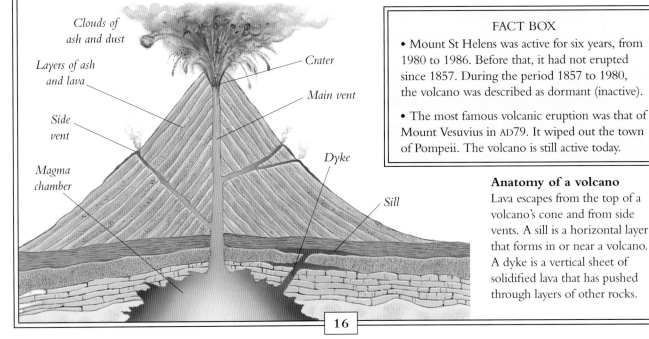

Clouds of ash and dust

Layers of ash and lava

Side vent

Magma chamber

Crater

Main vent

Dyke

Sill

FACT BOX
• Mount St Helens was active for six years, from 1980 to 1986. Before that, it had not erupted since 1857. During the period 1857 to 1980, the volcano was described as dormant (inactive).

• The most famous volcanic eruption was that of Mount Vesuvius in AD79. It wiped out the town of Pompeii. The volcano is still active today.

Anatomy of a volcano
Lava escapes from the top of a volcano's cone and from side vents. A sill is a horizontal layer that forms in or near a volcano. A dyke is a vertical sheet of solidified lava that has pushed through layers of other rocks.

Basalt

Pumice

Obsidian

Lava

Lava flowers

Volcanic rocks

A variety of rocks are formed by volcanoes. Basalt is formed by smooth, flowing lava. Gas bubbles trapped in the basalt form rock with lots of holes. Obsidian forms when sticky magma, rich in silica, violently erupts, then rapidly cools. Lava flowers form as minerals crystallize near volcanic springs.

Floating rock

Where frothy lava cools above ground, it forms a rock called pumice. Bubbles of gas are trapped inside pumice, making it very light for its size. This is why it floats on water. Pumice stone can be used in the bath to rub away dry skin.

Plug mountain

This impressive peak is a volcanic plug in Warrumbungle National Park, Australia. Magma that solidifies underground forms tough plugs. These are sometimes left behind as rocks around them are lost, worn away by the sea, rain or wind.

Rivers of lava

Liquid lava that flows from an active volcano appears red. This is because it is red hot. The lava often forms rivers that can form new land as they flow into the sea. On land, lava flows can start fires in forests and endanger people's lives.

IGNEOUS ROCKS

IGNEOUS rocks start off deep within the Earth as magma (molten rock) – giving them the name igneous, which means "of fire". The magma rises towards the surface where it may erupt from a volcano, or cool and solidify within the Earth's crust. Igneous rocks that form above ground are called extrusive and are usually associated with volcanoes. Rocks that form underground are called intrusive rocks. The magma that forms intrusive rocks solidifies slowly, allowing large crystals to form. Such rocks are usually coarse-grained, because of these large crystals. Granite is a common example of an intrusive igneous rock. Where magma solidifies below the surface, it often forms solid plugs of granite that may be several kilometres thick and just as wide. These are called plutons.

Rocks for tools
This Stone Age axe is made of rhyolite, an igneous rock that has razor-sharp edges.

The Granite City
Granite is hard-wearing, and carves well, making it a good building material. Many of the buildings in Aberdeen, Scotland, are made of granite.

Coarse-grained granite
This sample of granite is typical of igneous rocks. You can see the grainy texture, caused by the crystals that grew as the magma solidified to form the rock.

Fine-grained basalt
Basalt is the most common extrusive igneous rock. Because basalt cooled quickly above ground, its crystal grains are smaller and the rock looks and feels smoother than granite.

Glassy obsidian
When magma cools very rapidly, the atoms or molecules are not able to join together in a regular pattern to form crystals. Instead, they form a glassy material, such as obsidian.

Half Dome

Millions of years ago, a huge dome of magma intruded under what is now Yosemite National Park in California. It slowly cooled to form granite. The rocks around it were worn away by glaciers, leaving these dome-shaped hills behind.

Granite tors

Tors are typical granite landforms that look like huge boulders stacked one on top of the other. Because granite is a very hard, weather-resistant rock, tors remain when the surrounding rock is worn away. This tor is on Dartmoor in England.

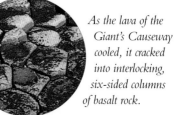

As the lava of the Giant's Causeway cooled, it cracked into interlocking, six-sided columns of basalt rock.

Giant's Causeway

The impressive columns of the Giant's Causeway in Northern Ireland are solid basalt. As lava reached the surface, it flowed into the sea, where it cooled and split into mainly hexagonal (six-sided) columns. The minerals that make up basalt, such as feldspars, pyroxenes and olivine, typically make the rock dark grey to black.

MAKING IGNEOUS ROCKS

THE projects on these pages will show you how igneous rocks can be grainy and made of large crystals, or smooth and glassy. You will be melting sugar, then letting it solidify. Sugar melts at a low enough temperature for you to experiment safely. If you used real magma, you would need to heat it up to around 1,000°C (1,800°F)! Even with sugar, the temperature is high, so take care while you carry out these projects, with the help of an adult. You can also make the sugar mixture into bubbly honeycomb, a form similar to pumice. It is like pumice because hundreds of tiny bubbles are captured inside the hot sugar.

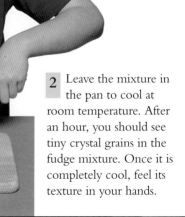

Honeycomb (pumice)

Toffee (obsidian)

Fudge (granite)

Fudge's grainy texture is similar to granite. Like obsidian, glassy toffee cools too rapidly to form crystals. The bubbles in 'honeycomb' are like pumice.

MATERIALS

You will need: sugar, water, large pan, safety glasses, wooden spoon, milk.

Making crystalline rock

1 Ask an adult to heat 500g (1lb) of sugar with a little water in a pan. Heat until the mixture turns brown, not black, then add a dash of milk.

2 Leave the mixture in the pan to cool at room temperature. After an hour, you should see tiny crystal grains in the fudge mixture. Once it is completely cool, feel its texture in your hands.

Making glass and bubbles

1 Spread butter over a metal baking tray. Put in the freezer for at least an hour to get very cold. Wearing oven mitts, remove from the freezer.

M A T E R I A L S

2 Ask an adult to heat about 500g (1lb) of sugar with a little water in a pan. The sugar dissolves in the water, but the water soon evaporates.

You will need: butter, baking parchment, baking tray, oven mitts, sugar, water, large pan, wooden spoon, safety glasses, bicarbonate of soda (baking soda).

3 The sugar mixture should be stirred while it heats up. Make sure that the sugar does not burn and turn black.

Bicarbonate gives off the gas carbon dioxide to form tiny bubbles.

5 To make 'honeycomb', stir in a spoonful of bicarbonate of soda in Step 3, just before you pour the sugar on to the tray.

4 Pour the mixture on to the cool baking tray. In ten minutes, the glassy and brittle toffee should have cooled enough for you to pick up.

SEDIMENTARY ROCKS

ANY of the most familiar rocks are sedimentary rocks. These form as sand, mud or other small rock particles settle in layers and then harden over thousands of years. The small pieces of rock are called sediment when they are carried along by water in rivers or the sea. Sediment forms because other rocks are eroded (worn down) by rain, wind, waves or huge rivers of ice called glaciers. Sedimentary rocks form where rivers meet the sea, or in shallow lakes where there is a limit to the amount of sediment the water can hold. Lakes of salty water evaporate to form rock salt, a sedimentary rock made largely of the same type of salt that we use to season our food.

Sandstone monolith
Uluru (Ayers Rock) is a monolith (huge block of stone) in central Australia. It is the remains of a vast sandstone formation that once covered the entire region.

Clay
The particles in clay are too fine even to see with a microscope. Clay absorbs water, which makes it pliable.

Chalk
A pure form of limestone, chalk is made from the skeletons of millions of tiny sea creatures.

Limestone
This is one of the commonest sedimentary rocks. It forms in water and consists mainly of the mineral calcite.

Conglomerate
A conglomerate contains rounded pebbles or shells, cemented together by rock made of much smaller particles.

Sandstone
There are many types of sandstone, each one made of tiny grains cemented together. The grains are usually quartz.

Red sandstone
The grains in this rock are coated with the mineral hematite (iron oxide). This makes it look red.

Beach pebbles

To see how the particles in sedimentary rocks form, look at the different sizes of pebble on a beach. The constant motion of the waves grinds the pebbles smaller and smaller. When they settle and the conditions are right, these particles will form sedimentary rock.

Rock salt pillars

The salt that forms rock salt is a chemical compound called sodium chloride, or halite. Rock salt forms as water evaporates from a salt solution, such as seawater. Here, pillars have formed in the extremely salty water of the Dead Sea, on the border of Israel and Jordan.

The red coloration of this halite is caused by impurities.

As water dries out, rock salt forms in pillars at the lake's edge

Meeting place

Many sedimentary rocks form at deltas, where a river meets the sea. The river's flow slows right down, so sediment can no longer be held in the water and is deposited. This picture of a delta on the island of Madagascar was taken by satellite.

ROCKS IN LAYERS

SEDIMENTARY rocks form as small particles of rock accumulate at the bottom of seas and lakes, or in deserts. These particles settle to cover large areas and, over thousands or millions of years, new layers of sediment are laid down on top of existing ones. So, most sedimentary rocks form in layers, called strata. The strata that are deepest underground are the oldest, because more recent layers are laid down on top of them. For this reason, sedimentary rock strata can provide valuable clues about the distant history of the Earth. Once sedimentary rocks have been formed, they may be subject to powerful forces caused by the movement of the Earth's crust. These forces cause folds or faults in the strata, which are often visible in rock faces.

Strata sandwich
A multi-layer sandwich is like rock strata. The first layer is a slice of bread at the bottom. Each filling is laid on top with more slices of bread. When it is cut through you can see the many different layers.

Layers of rock
Splits in the ground reveal sedimentary rock strata. Here you can see many different layers, with the oldest rocks at the bottom. Each layer is a different type of rock, suggesting that conditions in this region changed many times in the past.

Folding strata
This rock face shows what happens when parts of the Earth's crust are pushed together. Experts call downward folds synforms and upward folds antiforms. Some mountain ranges are formed by large-scale folding.

Geological time chart
The Earth's history is divided into eras, periods and epochs.

Era	Period		Million years ago
Cenozoic	**Quaternary**		
	Holocene (epoch)		0.01
	Pleistocene (epoch)		2
	Neogene		
	Pliocene (epoch)		5
	Miocene (epoch)		25
	Palaeogene		
	Oligocene (epoch)		38
	Eocene (epoch)		55
	Palaeocene (epoch)		65
Mesozoic	**Cretaceous**		144
	Jurassic		213
	Triassic		248
Paleozoic	**Permian**		286
	Carboniferous		360
	Devonian		408
	Silurian		438
	Ordovician		505
	Cambrian		590
Precambrian			4,600

Breaking the record
Often two strata of sedimentary rock look very different from each other. This is evidence of a break in the layers of strata, perhaps because mountains formed. Often there is a big gap in age between the older and younger rocks.

Grand Canyon
The 1.6 km (1 mile) deep Grand Canyon, in Arizona, USA, was cut by the Colorado River, revealing cliff faces with impressive strata. Those at the bottom are more than 2,000 million years old. Those at the top are about 60 million years old.

MAKING SEDIMENTARY ROCKS

To help you understand the processes by which sedimentary rocks are made and how they form distinct layers called strata, you can make your own sedimentary rocks. Different strata of rock are laid down by different types of sediment, so the first project involves making strata of your own, using various things found around the kitchen. The powerful forces that move parts of the Earth's crust often cause strata to fold, fault or just tilt and you can see this, too. In the second project, you can make a copy of a type of sedimentary rock called a conglomerate, in which small pebbles and sand become cemented into a finer material. Conglomerates in nature can be found in areas that were once underwater.

The finished jar of strata imitates real rock strata. Sediments are always laid down flat, but the forces that shape the land can tilt or fold strata as here.

M A T E R I A L S

You will need: large jar, modelling clay, spoon, flour, kidney beans, brown sugar, rice, lentils (or similar ingredients).

Making your own strata

1 Press one edge of the jar into a piece of modelling clay, so that the jar sits at an angle. Slowly pour a layer of flour about 2cm (1in) thick into the jar.

2 Carefully make alternate layers with kidney beans, brown sugar, rice, lentils and flour, building them up nearly to the top of the jar.

3 Remove the jar from the clay and stand it upright.

Making conglomerate rock

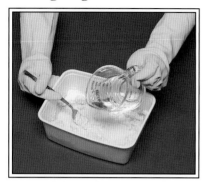

1 Put on a pair of rubber gloves. In an old container, make up some plaster of Paris with water, following the instructions on the packet.

2 Mix in small pebbles, sand and soil into the plaster of Paris. Mix them in well, to make sure they are evenly distributed.

3 Leave the mixture for ten minutes, until it starts to harden, then press a small lump of it into a ball shape in your hand.

M A T E R I A L S

You will need: rubber gloves, old container, plaster of Paris, water, fork or spoon, pebbles, sand, soil, waste paper.

Finished rocks

4 Make some more conglomerate rocks in different sizes with different amounts of pebbles in. Place the rocks on a spare piece of paper to harden and dry out completely.

Real rock
Do your rocks look anything like this boulder of real conglomerate rock? The many fragments in this boulder vary a great deal in size and coloration.

OUR CHANGING EARTH

THE crust of the Earth is composed of several enormous pieces rather like the shell of a cracked egg. These pieces are called plates and are moving. They are pushed apart as new rocks form at the boundaries between the plates. These new rocks form as magma leaks out from the Earth's mantle, at places called oceanic ridges. At other boundaries, plates are being pushed together. Boundaries where one plate is forced underneath the other are called subduction zones. The study of the plates and their movement is called plate tectonics. It has helped to explain many features of the Earth's landscape, such as the formation of mountain ranges. Plate tectonics can also explain why earthquakes happen.

Plates and earthquakes
On this map, you can see the major plates of the Earth's crust. Also marked are the sites of frequent earthquakes. Earthquake sites lie in belts that usually follow the edges of the Earth's tectonic plates.

A pattern of lines
If you mark the sites of the world's active volcanoes on a map, you will find that they occur in lines. These lines are actually along the boundaries between two plates.

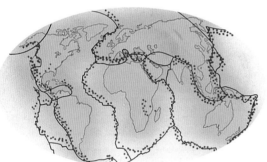

The ocean floor
At an oceanic ridge, plates move apart creating new crust. This movement also creates subduction zones, where one plate is pushed underneath another. Where plates collide, oceanic crust is always forced under continental crust. Rock melts as it is forced down, but some pushes to the surface to form volcanoes. New mountain chains form where plates collide.

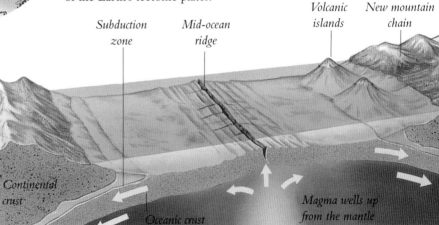

Subduction zone
Mid-ocean ridge
Volcanic islands
New mountain chain
Continental crust
Oceanic crust
Magma wells up from the mantle

Black smokers
At oceanic ridges, hot mineral-rich water formed by the molten rock streams from cracks. These underwater springs are sometimes called black smokers. Strange, large, red-lipped worms and white crabs live near these vents.

The San Andreas Fault
Some plates slip sideways past each other. That is what is happening at the San Andreas Fault, California. The two plates move about 6cm (2.5in) past each other every year. This movement causes earthquakes and tremors, especially in the nearby city of San Francisco.

FACT BOX
• The continents on either side of the Atlantic Ocean are moving apart 2.5cm (1in) per year. In the middle of the Atlantic is an oceanic ridge some 16,000km (10,000 miles) long.

• In 1912, Alfred Wegener noted that the continents almost fit together like a jigsaw. He proposed that the continents are drifting apart. The theory of plate tectonics arose from this movement, called continental drift.

Earthquake!
Where plates rub against each other, they do so with enormous force, producing massive vibrations in the ground. The vibrations may be violent enough to shake or even destroy buildings. Buildings in cities at risk often have to be earthquake-proof.

METAMORPHIC ROCKS

THE word metamorphic means "changed" and that is exactly what these rocks are. Metamorphic rocks form when igneous or sedimentary rocks are subjected to high temperatures or crushed by huge pressures underground. This changes the properties and the appearance of the rocks. For example, the sedimentary rock limestone becomes marble. There are two types of metamorphism. In contact metamorphism, molten magma from the Earth's mantle pushes its way up into the rocks of the crust. The rocks that surround the intruding magma are heated by the hot magma. In regional metamorphism, rocks are heated as they are buried and squeezed as they are pushed together in the middle of mountain ranges.

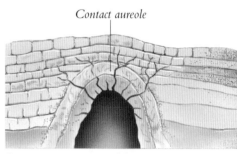
Contact aureole

Contact metamorphism
This type of metamorphism happens in what is called a contact aureole – the area around an intrusion of magma. Heat from the magma bakes the surrounding rocks, altering their form and composition.

The minerals form in bands, giving a foliated (layered) appearance.

Gneiss
Under very high temperature and pressure, many igneous or sedimentary rocks can become gneiss *(pronounced "nice")*. All gneisses are made of bands of minerals. In some, each band is a different mineral. In others they are different-sized crystals of the same mineral.

The mineral olivine gives this marble its green shade. The rest is mostly calcite.

Marble
When heat and pressure alter limestone, a very common sedimentary rock, marble forms. Impurities in the limestone give marble its varied coloration, with red, yellow, brown, blue, grey and green, arranged in veins or patterns.

Mica crystals in slate give it a shiny, wet appearance.

Slate
This rock is formed from mudstone or shale, which are made from tiny particles of clay. Slate forms at a relatively low temperature. Because of this, fossils from the original rocks often survive in slate.

Roofing slates

One of the main uses of slate is as a covering for roofs. To make roofing slates, blocks of the rock are first hit lightly with a chisel in several places. The rock splits naturally along lines within the rock's structure, forming thin sheets.

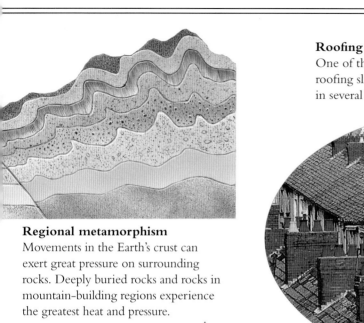

Regional metamorphism

Movements in the Earth's crust can exert great pressure on surrounding rocks. Deeply buried rocks and rocks in mountain-building regions experience the greatest heat and pressure.

The Taj Mahal

Marble is used for impressive buildings, such as the Taj Mahal in India. Pure white marble is one of the most prized stones for building and carving.

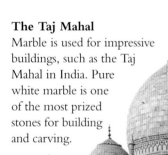

Marble is hard wearing and has a translucent quality that gives it a characteristic sheen.

Marble inlay

Marble is very attractive when it is cut and polished. The intricate inlaid pattern on this building is made from marble and other stones. Marble has been prized by artists and architects since ancient times.

MOVING PLATES

A s the plates of the Earth collide at subduction zones with great force, some heat is generated by friction (rubbing) on faults. You can experience this by simply rubbing your own hands together. The plates of the Earth's crust are floating on the mantle underneath. Oceanic crust always floats lower than continental crust, which is why oceanic crust is always pushed underneath continental crust at subduction zones. The reason oceanic crust floats lower is that it is more dense (heavier for the same size) than continental crust. You can see how this works in the first project below, which compares the densities of two objects. In the second project, you can see how movements in the Earth's crust, caused by the moving plates, have created different landforms. These landforms include mountains, block mountains and rift valleys.

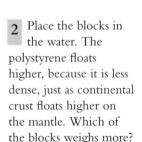

Friction rub
Experience the heat of friction by rubbing your hands together. The harder you rub, the more heat you produce.

You will need: block of wood, polystyrene or styrofoam block, bowl, water.

Floating high and low

1 You will need two blocks, one of wood to be oceanic crust and one of polystyrene to be continental crust. They must be the same size and shape. Half-fill a bowl with water to represent the fluid mantle.

2 Place the blocks in the water. The polystyrene floats higher, because it is less dense, just as continental crust floats higher on the mantle. Which of the blocks weighs more?

Building mountains

1 Roll out several flat sheets of modelling clay, each one a different shade. The sheets should be about 20cm (8in) square.

2 Place the squares on top of each other to make a layered block, like layers of rock strata in the continental crust.

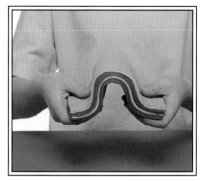

3 Push your block from both ends. The block folds, forming a fold mountain. Real fold mountains are formed from strata in this way.

M A T E R I A L S

You will need: different shades of modelling clay, rolling pin, 20cm (8in) square sheet of paper, modelling tool.

Block mountains

Rift valley

Uplifted rock strata form block mountains, while a descending mass of rock creates a rift valley.

4 Make another block of stratified modelling clay as in Steps 1 and 2 above. Carefully make two cuts in the clay with a modelling tool.

5 Lift up the outside pieces to form block mountains separated by a rift valley. The crust breaks in this way at a rift zone, where plates are moving apart.

GEOLOGISTS AT WORK

GEOLOGY is the study of the history of the Earth, as told by the rocks found in the Earth's crust. Scientists who study geology are called geologists. Some geologists specialize in certain branches of geology. For example, paleontologists study fossils, mineralogists specialize in identifying minerals and those who study the structure and composition of rocks are called petrologists. Most geologists spend some of their time in the field, collecting samples. The rest of their time is spent in laboratories, analysing the samples they have collected. There are many methods used by geologists to identify samples of rocks and the minerals of which they are made. One important method is to find their density, which is different for different minerals. Once a geologist has identified a set of rock samples and worked out the ages of the rocks, he or she can produce a geological map of the area from which they came.

Geological map
A geological map is used to search for oil, which is often found in certain rocks and rock structures. Architects also look at an area's geology before they plan a building project.

Fieldwork
These geologists are sampling water from a volcanic spring. Most geologists carry out fieldwork like this. They spend time studying rocks where they are found on the Earth's surface.

Sampling gas
These geologists are collecting samples of gas given off by a volcano. They wear gas masks, because some of the gases may be harmful to their health.

Geological hammer

Hammers are used to collect samples of rock. They also act as a size and direction guide when photographed in position.

Density

These two blocks are the same size and shape, but do not weigh the same. The materials they are made of have different densities. Density is used to identify minerals, since samples of the same mineral will have the same density.

FACT BOX

• After rocks have been formed, radioactive elements in some minerals change gradually, over thousands of years, into other elements. By measuring the amounts of those elements geologists can calculate a rock's age.

• Another way to tell the age of rocks is to look at the fossils they contain. Different plants and animals lived at different times in the past. Identifying fossils can tell you where in the geological record a rock fits.

Micrograph

A micrograph is a photograph taken through a microscope. This picture shows the grains in sandstone greatly magnified. Grain size and shape can help to identify sandstones.

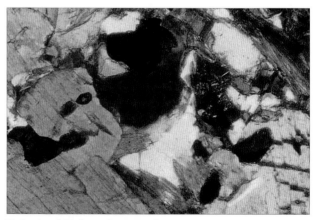

Polarized light micrograph

This micrograph is of a thin section of a metamorphic rock called schist. It reveals the crystals of different minerals that make up the rock, helping to identify its origin and the conditions of temperature and pressure when it formed.

IDENTIFYING MINERALS

GEOLOGISTS use many different methods to identify the minerals that make up rocks. Each mineral possesses a unique set of identifying properties. Geologists use several tests to identify minerals, such as hardness (how easily a mineral scratches), specific gravity (comparing a mineral's density to the density of water), streak (the shade of a mineral's powder), lustre (the way light reflects off the surface), transparency (whether light can pass through or not) and coloration (some minerals are a distinctive shade in natural light).

Dropping acid on to a sample to see if gas is given off is a simple test that can be carried out in the field. You can also try simple versions of two tests that geologists use. They will help you identify some samples that you have collected. Firstly, rubbing a rock on to the back of a tile leaves a streak mark – the coloration of the streak can reveal what minerals are present. Then you can calculate the specific gravity of a sample.

Acid test
Drop a rock into vinegar. If gas bubbles form, it contains minerals called carbonates (e.g. calcite).

You will need: a white tile, several samples of different rocks or minerals, field guide.

Streak test

1 Place a tile face down, so that the rough side is facing upwards. Choose one of your samples and rub it against the tile. You should see a streak appear on the tile's surface.

2 Make streaks using the other samples and compare coloration. Rocks made of several minerals may leave several different streaks.

Specific gravity test

1 Choose a rock and weigh it as accurately as you can to find its mass. The figure should be in grams. Make a note of the mass.

2 Fill a clear measuring jug or cup to the 200ml mark with water. Now carefully place the first rock sample into the water.

3 Look carefully at the scale on the jug to read off the new water level. Make a note of the level of the water in your notebook.

MATERIALS

You will need: mineral or rock samples, accurate metric weighing scales, notebook, pen or pencil, measuring jug or cup, water.

The mass of a sample divided by its volume gives you its density, or specific gravity.

4 Subtract 200 from the figure you wrote down in Step 3. This is the sample's volume in millilitres. Now divide the mass (weight) by the volume to find the density. You can use a calculator to do this sum if you wish.

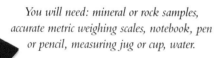

Pyrite   *Beryl*

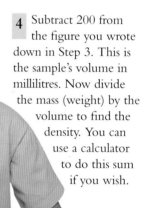

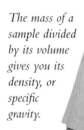

More dense

If a mineral has a specific gravity (SG) of 5, it is five times as dense as water. Pyrite has an SG of 5 and beryl has an SG of 2.6. The atoms in pyrite are more closely packed together, making it denser.

WEARING AWAY

The rocks of the Earth's crust are constantly being worn away in a process called erosion. There are several causes of erosion, such as glaciers, water (rain, rivers and the sea), wind and changes in temperature. A glacier is like a huge river of ice, and the weight of the ice scrapes the surface of the rock away. When it rains, the minerals in some rocks dissolve into the rainwater and are washed away into rivers. Particles of sand, or other material carried by strong winds, can grind a rock down like wind-blown sandpaper. When the temperature falls below freezing, water in the small gaps of a rock freezes. Water expands as it freezes and this freeze-thaw erosion can literally shatter rocks apart.

Ice power
As water freezes it expands. Water in cracks can split a rock apart as it turns to ice.

Large and small
Grains of sand start off as large chunks of rock. As the sea moves in waves, the rocks rub against each other and are worn down into round and smooth pebbles. After years of erosion, these get smaller and smaller and end up as tiny grains of sand.

River of ice
A glacier creeps along a handsbreadth each day, the ice gouging out the rock beneath it. Large, flat-bottomed valleys are common in locations where glaciers once existed, but retreated long ago.

Natural arch bridge
Arches have formed in this headland. Waves bend round the headland as they approach the shore. Over centuries, the force of the water wears away the middle.

Sand-blown canyon

Sculpted by the wind, this canyon in Utah, USA, is made of sandstone. Its carved walls are the result of constant erosion by wind-blown sand slowly grinding away at the rock.

Monument Valley

The strangely-shaped rocks in Monument Valley, Arizona, USA, were also carved by the wind. It wore away the softer layers of rock producing isolated flat-topped hills called buttes.

Erosion by rain

The Badlands of South Dakota, USA, have been eroded into hills and gullies by rainwater. The characteristic shapes are carved out of the desert by flash floods that occur after torrential desert rainfall. Floods sweep down the gullies, tearing down slopes, undermining cliffs and dislodging boulders.

LIMESTONE LANDSCAPES

Limestone

Calcite

Flint nodule

The main mineral in limestone is calcite, which dissolves easily. Lumps of flint (a form of quartz) are often found in limestones.

LIMESTONE is a very common sedimentary rock, made largely of a mineral called calcite. The rock forms particularly interesting landscapes, because calcite dissolves quite easily in water. So, where rivers flow above or below ground, through regions of limestone, distinctive shapes are formed. Caves are a common feature of limestone landscapes. They are formed when slightly acidic rainwater dissolves large volumes of rock underground. Where water drips from rocks inside caves, some dissolved calcite is deposited (left behind) forming pillars called stalactites and stalagmites. In many limestone landscapes, especially where rainfall is fairly high, particular scenery called karst is found. Another rock that consists largely of calcite is travertine. Like stalagmites and stalactites, it forms when calcite is deposited by water but here around streams and waterfalls. It creates some unusual landscapes.

Karst scenery
These pinnacles are in Australia's Blue Mountains. Limestone areas create spectacular landscapes, called karst. Rainwater runs through cracks in the limestone to form underground caves and large holes called sink holes. Where the strata are tilted, deep cracks create pinnacles.

Limestone cones
Cones of limestone rock rise from beside the Li Jiang river near Guilin, China. The strange and beautiful towers were formed by intense downward erosion by rain and river water.

Limestone pavement

In many limestone regions, large flat pavements of jointed blocks are formed. Rainwater flows into cracks in the rock, dissolving the calcite and producing deep narrow cracks called grikes.

Travertine

This famous terraced landscape is the Pamukkale Falls, in Turkey. Calcite from hot springs deposits travertine in beautifully shaped terraces over thousands of years. Travertine is quarried and used as a decorative building stone.

Inside a cave

Stalactites grow down from the roof of a cave. The drips that form them land on the ground and form upward-pointing spikes called stalagmites. Where stalactites and stalagmites meet, a column forms. These spectacular rock formations are part of the Carlsbad Caves in New Mexico, USA.

LOOKING AT EROSION

You will need: sand, water, baking tray, brick, deeper tray or bowl.

THE shape of much of the land around us is created by erosion. You can get a feel for some of the processes of erosion with a few simple experiments. In the projects on these pages, you will be able to see how the flow of water can create familiar landscapes. In the first project, you may even be able to produce a natural arch bridge in a sand castle. The next project looks at one result of erosion in limestone landscapes – the formation of hard water, which contains dissolved minerals. If you evaporate the water, it will leave behind the minerals it contains. By doing this you can compare the hardness of different water samples. In the last project on these pages, you can experiment with chemical erosion, which is also called weathering. This occurs when minerals dissolve in a liquid, such as rainwater. This project uses sugar, because it dissolves easily in water.

To make the sand castle, dampen the sand with a little water beforehand. This will make it stick together better.

Shaping the land

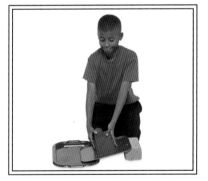

2 Drip water on to the castle. Watch it crumble and form a new shape as the sand erodes away where the water hits it.

1 Put one end of the baking tray on a brick so that it slopes down towards a deeper tray or bowl. Make a sand castle on the baking tray.

3 If you make the water flow down the baking tray so that it hits the middle of the sand castle, you may be able to erode the middle part, leaving a natural arch. Here the arch has eroded so much it has collapsed.

Hard water

1 Fill three foil trays or saucers with the same amount of water – one with mineral water, one with tap water and one with distilled water.

2 Label the trays and leave them somewhere warm and well-ventilated. Try to be sure that they will not be disturbed for a few days.

Distilled

Tap

3 When it has evaporated, the water should leave behind any minerals. Which sample contained most dissolved minerals?

Mineral

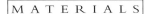

M A T E R I A L S

You will need: three small foil trays or saucers, mineral water, tap water, distilled water, labels, pen.

Chemical erosion

1 Build a pile of brown sugar on a tray. Imagine that it is a mountain made of a soluble rock (dissolving in water). Press the sugar down firmly.

M A T E R I A L S

You will need: baking tray, brown sugar, water.

2 Drip water on the mountain. It will be eroded as the sugar dissolves in the water. The water running off should be brown, because it contains dissolved brown sugar.

SAND AND SOIL

To a geologist, sand is any collection of grains of rock between 0.02 and 2mm in diameter. It is formed by the erosion of rocks in several different environments. On beaches and in rivers, for example, the erosion is caused by the movement of the water. Desert sand is produced by wind blowing small rock particles against each other so that they become ground down into smaller and smaller pieces. Geologists can tell how the grains in sandstone were formed by looking at the distinctive shapes of the grains. Soil is formed in similar ways to sand by the erosion of rocks, but there is an important difference. Soil contains organic matter – the remains of plants and animals. This organic matter forms humus, which mixes with rock particles and allows plants to grow in the soil.

Black sand
Not all sand is yellow. Any rock can form sand. The black sand on this beach is grains of basalt, a dark igneous rock formed from volcanic lava.

Sand dunes
In dry climates, where deserts form, sand is blown by the wind to form hills called dunes. Sand dunes reform and travel across the desert, blown by the wind. These red dunes are part of the Namib Desert in southwest Africa.

Sea mists provide enough moisture for some plants to survive

Barkhans are crescent-shaped dunes that are always moving

The wind creates beach-like ripples on the desert floor

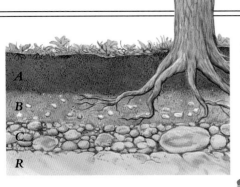

Dead leaves

As dead leaves and branches rot down they release nutrients back into the soil. Trees and other plants need these nutrients to grow.

Soil in layers

Soil occurs in layers, called horizons. There are four main horizons, called A, B, C and R. The A horizon (also called topsoil) is a layer of fine particles that supports the roots of plants and trees. In the layers beneath the topsoil, the soil particles become larger. The R horizon is partly solid rock.

As trees grow, their roots help break down rock into soil. The roots work into cracks, splitting a rock apart.

Oak seedling

Root tips grow down

Beach sand
Tiny particles of sand under a microscope. The grains have been smoothed and rounded by wave action. Rounded sand grains form sandstones.

Graded beds

Sand is moved along by flowing water. Where the current slows, sand and rock particles are deposited. This builds up layers of rock called a graded bed. Movements in the crust can tilt the bed at angles.

River sand
These coarser particles of sand are more typical of sand eroded in a river. Compacted together, they would form gritstone, a coarse type of sandstone.

WHAT IS SOIL MADE OF?

SAND and soil are made of millions of very small particles. Sand is formed from many types of rock, by a process called attrition, which means grinding down. Desert sand forms by attrition, as wind-blown sand rubs against rocks of all sizes. You can see how attrition forms small particles simply by shaking some sugar cubes together in a glass jar. Soil is also made of tiny particles, usually clay, along with dead plant and animal matter. In the first project, a sample of soil is examined, using a sieve to separate particles of different sizes. In the second project, you can find out how graded beds of sediment form in rivers, lakes and seas, as first large and then finer particles of sediment are deposited.

MATERIALS

You will need: gloves, trowel, old sieve or fine strainer, paper, notebook, magnifier, soil, pen or pencil.

Sugar shaker
Shake some sugar cubes in a jar. The cubes knock together as you shake. After a while you will see many tiny grains of sugar.

What is in soil?

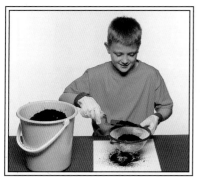

1 Put on the gloves and place a trowel full of soil into the sieve. Shake the sieve over a piece of white paper for a minute or so.

2 Tap the side of the sieve gently to help separate the different parts of the soil. Are there particles that will not go through the sieve?

3 Examine the soil particles that fall on to the paper, using a magnifier. Can you see any small living creatures?

Big or small?

1 Using scissors, cut off the top of a large, clear plastic bottle. Throw away the top part.

2 Put small stones or gravel, soil and sand into the bottom of the bottle. Add water nearly to the top.

3 Stir the stones, gravel, soil, sand and water vigorously. In a river, rock particles are mixed together and carried along by the moving water.

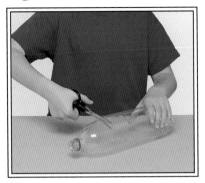

You will need: scissors, large clear plastic bottle, small stones or gravel, soil, sand, wooden spoon, water.

Sedimentary rocks often form in graded beds. This is because particles settle at different rates.

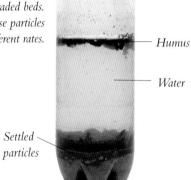

Humus — Water — Settled particles

Humus

An important constituent of soil is humus. This is produced by animals called decomposers, such as worms and woodlice. These animals eat dead plant and animal matter, including leaves. As the matter passes through their bodies, it is broken down in their digestive systems.

4 Leave the mixture to settle. You should find that the particles settle in different layers, with the heaviest particles at the bottom and the lightest on top.

THE COAL AGE

Peat

Brown coal

THE solid black material that we call coal is a very useful mineral. It is called a fossil fuel, because it was formed millions of years ago and its main use is as a fuel. It is burned in power stations to generate electricity. To some geologists, coal is not a mineral at all, because it was made from millions of dead plants (only non-living or inorganic materials are usually considered to be minerals). Coal is found between the strata of certain sedimentary rocks and is dug up in coal mines both on the surface and deep underground. Most coal formed from plants that lived and died in the Carboniferous period, between 286 and 360 million years ago. At that time, tropical rainforests existed across Europe, Asia and North America.

Lush rainforest
Damp, swampy rainforest is a similar environment to the one in which coal formed millions of years ago. To produce coal, the remains of plants lay submerged under water, in swamps or shallow lakes, for millions of years.

Black coal

Anthracite

Types of coal
The hardest, best quality coal is called anthracite. More crumbly black coal and lower grade brown coal (lignite) do not give as much energy when burned. Lignite is younger than black coal and anthracite. Peat is younger still. It forms constantly in boggy areas.

Bark fossil
This piece of coal clearly shows the bark patterns of the plant it came from. Plants such as tree-like horsetails, primitive conifers and giant ferns grew in huge forests.

Stoking up the fire
Coal releases large amounts of energy as heat when it burns. This steam locomotive uses heat from burning coal to produce steam to drive its wheels.

Since Bronze Age times, jet has been carved into many decorative objects. It was popular in Victorian Britain for mourning jewellery.

Victorian jet brooch

Black as jet
Jet is a material that is similar to coal. It is formed from driftwood that had settled in mud at the bottom of the ocean. It is very light and can be polished and carved.

Natural jet

At the coal face
Most coal is mined underground. Tunnels are built so that people and machines can reach an exposed seam of coal, called the coal face. In difficult to reach areas, the coal must be mined by hand.

Coal-fired power station
Power stations are often near coal fields. Coal is used to heat water to make steam. Steam-driven turbines run huge generators that produce electricity for homes and factories.

PRESERVED IN STONE

THE shapes of some organisms (plants and animals) that died millions of years ago have been preserved in rock as fossils. After an organism dies, sediments may form around its remains. This is particularly true if the organism died in water. Slowly, over thousands of years, the sediments compact together to form sedimentary rock. The organic remains themselves disintegrate, but minerals from the rocks may take the place of the bones or the outline of an animal's body. Minerals can also replace the stem, leaves and flowers of a plant. The rock strata in which a fossil is found are a key to the environment in which the organism lived. The study of fossils, called paleontology, tells us much about how life evolved, both in the sea and on

Coccosphere

Radiolaria

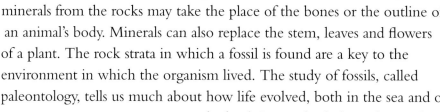

Foraminifera

Microfossils

Just as there are living organisms too small to see without a microscope (microorganisms) there are also microfossils. These fossils are tiny marine organisms that lived during the Cretaceous period (about 65 to 144 million years ago). Millions of their remains are found in the sedimentary rock, chalk.

the land. It can also help to date rocks. Amber is also a fossil. It is the fossilized resin (a thick, sticky liquid) of trees similar to conifers that died millions of years ago. The resin slowly hardened and turned to stone. Insects sometimes became trapped in the resin and so were preserved inside the amber.

How fossils are formed

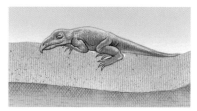

An animal or plant dies and falls on to the sand at the bottom of the ocean or into mud or sand on land. The water or mud protects the body.

The soft parts of the body rot away, but the bones and teeth remain. The body is covered with layers of mud, sand or other sediment.

Rocks form from the sediment. The hard parts are gradually replaced by minerals and fossilized. As the rocks above erode away, the fossil is revealed.

Ammonite

Amber

Types of fossils

Four common fossils are shown here. Fossils of sea creatures are often found, because their bodies cannot decay completely underwater. Ammonites were hard-shelled sea creatures that lived between 60 and 400 million years ago. Amber is the fossilized resin of 60 million-year-old trees. The leaf imprint formed in mudstone around 250 million years ago, and fern-like fossils are often found in coal.

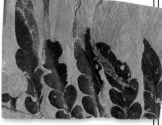

Leaf

Fern

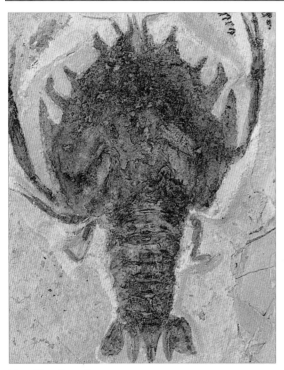

Fossilized crab
This crab lived in the ocean around 150 million years ago. Marine limestones (such as chalk), shales and marine sandstones contain the most fossils.

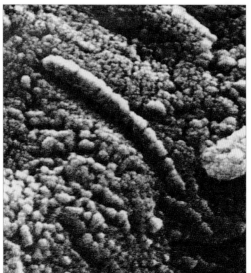

Martian fossils?
In 1996, scientists discovered what looked like tiny fossilized creatures in a rock that had originated on Mars. Everyone was excited about the possible proof that life had once existed on the planet, but it turned out that the marks were probably not fossils at all.

MAKING FOSSILS

Y OU cannot make a real fossil, because the process takes many thousands of years. However, these projects will help you to understand how two types of fossil came to exist. One type forms when a dead plant or animal leaves a space in the sedimentary rocks that come together around them. This is usually how the soft parts of an animal or a delicate leaf are preserved before they decay. The space in the rock is an imprint of the dead plant or animal. You can make a fossil of this kind using a shell, in the first project. In this case the shell does not decay – you simply remove it from the plaster. In another kind of fossil, the spaces formed by decaying parts of an animal's body or skeleton are filled with minerals. This gives a solid fossil that is a copy of the original body part. Make this kind of fossil in the second project.

M A T E R I A L S

You will need: plastic tub, plaster of Paris, water, fork, strip of paper, paper clip, modelling clay, shell, safety glasses, wooden board, hammer, chisel.

These are the finished results of the two projects. While you are making them, try to imagine how rocks form around real fossils. They are imprints of organisms that fell into mud millions of years ago.

Making a fossil imprint

1 In a plastic tub, mix up the plaster of Paris with water following the instructions on the packet. Make sure the mixture is fairly firm.

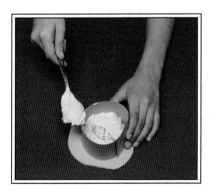

2 Fix the strip of paper into a collar with the paper clip. Make a base from modelling clay and press in the shell. Surround the shell with plaster.

3 Leave your plaster rock to dry for at least half an hour. With the help of an adult, crack open the rock and remove the shell to reveal the fossil imprint.

Making a solid fossil

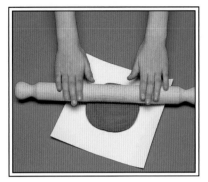

1 Put down a spare piece of paper to protect your work surface. Roll out a flat circle of modelling clay, about 2cm (1 inch) thick.

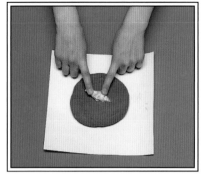

2 Press your shell or other object deep into the clay to leave a clear impression. Do not press it all the way to the paper at the bottom.

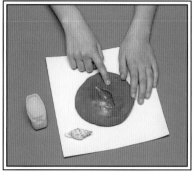

3 Remove the shell and lightly rub some petroleum jelly all over the shell impression. This will help you to remove the plaster fossil later.

MATERIALS

You will need: spare paper, rolling pin, modelling clay, shell, petroleum jelly, paper clip, strip of paper, glass, plaster of Paris, water, fork.

The bones of a dinosaur would leave a space like this impression in the rocks around them.

5 Now, carefully remove the solid plaster from your clay circle. When paleontologists find fossilized bones or teeth, they remove them very carefully from the surrounding rock. They do so in order not to damage their finds.

4 With the paper clip, fix the paper strip into a collar for the clay circle. Mix up some plaster of Paris, pour it in and leave to dry for half an hour.

USEFUL ROCKS

ROCKS are used to build houses, bridges and other stable structures. Building materials may be cut from large or small stones, or processed to make bricks. Another very important building material is concrete, which is made from cement. The cement is made from the sedimentary rock, limestone. Harder rocks, such as the igneous rock granite or the metamorphic rock marble, can be polished to a shiny finish and are used to make a beautiful decorative surface. It is not just in construction that rocks are used. Glass and other ceramics are made from rocks, by treating them with heat and the action of other chemicals. Rocks have been used as tools and weapons since the first human beings appeared on Earth over two and a half million years ago.

Strong shape
The weight of all the stones in this Medieval tower squashes the stones together, forming a strong, stable structure. Stone towers like this still stand today, over 550 years after they were built.

Axe

Scraper

Spear

Arrow

Spear

Chopper

The CN tower in Toronto, Canada

Reinforced concrete
Concrete consists of aggregate (sand and gravel) stuck together with cement (a mixture of limestone and clay). When reinforced with steel, it can be used for high-rise towers and skyscrapers that would otherwise have been impossible to build.

Flint tools
Among the first tools made by humans were stone hand axes and blades. One common material for early tool-making was flint. It fractures easily to give a sharp edge and could be flaked to form many different tools.

Yellow sulphur growing on kaolin

Lime

Soda ash

Sand

Decorative glazes used on porcelain are also made of minerals

Porcelain china

The most highly prized material for making crockery is ceramic porcelain. True porcelain is made using high-quality china clay, known as kaolin, which contains a silicate mineral called kaolinite. The word kaolin is from the name of a hill in China where the clay was first mined.

Making glass

Believe it or not, glass is made from sand. High-quality glass can be made by melting pure sand, but very high temperatures are needed. Most glass is made from sand mixed with soda ash and lime, a mixture that melts at a lower temperature. Glass was first made by the ancient Egyptians.

Building brick

Terracotta pot

Clay

FACT BOX

• In the mid-1700s, Coalbrookdale in England became one of the first industrial towns due to its interesting geology. It has an unusual sequence of rocks that includes layers of clay (for pottery and bricks) and coal, iron ore and limestone, which are the essential ingredients for iron-making. Running out of the rocks was natural bitumen, a material that was used to make machine oil. It was also used to waterproof the boats that transported the cast iron.

Shaping clay

When clay is mixed with water, it becomes malleable, which means that it can be shaped. Clay objects are first moulded, then placed in a kiln and heated until hard. Unglazed pottery made from red clay is called terracotta, which is from the Italian for "baked earth".

Marble slabs

Polished slabs of marble give an eye-catching surface used on floors and decorative objects. Stone workers call any attractive stone that can be cut and polished marble, although they are often only limestones and sometimes even granites.

METALS FROM ROCKS

MONG the most important rocks are metal ores. These contain minerals rich in metallic elements, such as iron, copper and tin. To make metal from an ore, the metal-rich mineral is first separated from the unwanted rock. To extract the metal from its mineral ore, the mineral is heated with various other substances in a process known as smelting. A few metals exist in rocks in their pure state. Gold is the best example of this and is found as veins and nuggets in many types of rock. Gold is dug from the rock in mines, although in some parts of the world it can be found as nuggets in rivers. Metals are very useful to people, because they are durable. They can be shaped into many objects and drawn out into a fine wire that will conduct (let through) heat and electricity. The first metal to be used on a large scale was copper, about 8,000 years ago.

Reclaimed by nature
Metals naturally exist bonded to other elements. Some readily rebond after extraction. Iron quickly joins with oxygen and water to form iron oxide, or rust.

Fine gold wires
Gold is a very important metal in the electronics industry. It is drawn out into thin wires that connect to microprocessors. Most metals can be drawn into fine wires – a property known as ductility. Gold is the most ductile of all metals. It also resists the corrosive effects of many chemicals.

Gold Rush
Sometimes rocks surrounding a nugget of gold are eroded by a river. Occasionally, the gold is released into the river and can be recovered by panning. This picture shows the 1849 Californian Gold Rush, when thousands hoped to make a fortune from gold.

Stainless steel cutlery

Hematite (iron ore)

Carbon

Iron

Atoms of iron exist in iron ore joined with atoms of oxygen. To produce iron metal, iron ore is heated in a furnace with carbon. The carbon takes away the oxygen atoms, leaving the metal behind. Adding more carbon produces steel, the most widely used metallic substance.

Copper pipes

Native copper

Copper

Water pipes and plastic-coated electrical wire are two of the biggest uses of copper. The metal is recovered from its ore by first removing impurities from the mineral, then heating it in a furnace with a blast of oxygen.

Bauxite (aluminium ore)

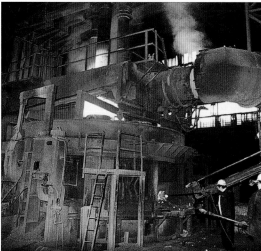

Aluminium foil

Aluminium

In aluminium ore (bauxite), aluminium atoms are joined to oxygen atoms. To remove the oxygen, electricity is passed through the ore.

Smelting iron

Iron ore is heated in a blast furnace to produce nearly pure iron. The blast furnace blows hot air through to remove impurities from the ore.

PRECIOUS STONES

Aboriginal Australians first drew rock paintings like this one thousands of years ago. They used earthy-toned mineral pigments, such as umber and ochre.

MINERALS that are highly prized for their beauty are called gemstones. The main use of gemstones is in jewellery or other decorative work, although some are also used in industry. Around 90 minerals are classed as gems, but only about 20 of these are important gems. These include diamonds, the most valuable of all gemstones. Some minerals provide more than one type of gem. For example, different types of the mineral beryl form emerald, aquamarine, heliodor and morganite. Gems such as ruby and emerald are distinctive because of their coloration. The different shades of gemstones are caused by metal impurities in the mineral. Other minerals, not necessarily gemstones, are prized for their coloration and are used as pigments. A small selection of gems is shown here.

Raw umber *Brown umber* *Yellow ochre*

Pigments

Minerals have been used for thousands of years as pigments. Rocks containing bright minerals are ground down, mixed with a binder, such as egg yolk, fat or oil, and used as paint.

Cameo

The gemstone agate occurs in layers of different shades. In a cameo, the top layer is carved to reveal the lower one as a background. This Greek cameo is of Alexander the Great.

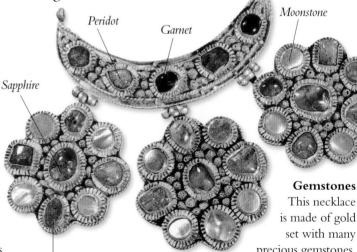

Peridot *Garnet* *Moonstone*

Sapphire

Pink sapphire

Gemstones

This necklace is made of gold set with many precious gemstones. Beautiful minerals have been used for thousands of years in ornamentation.

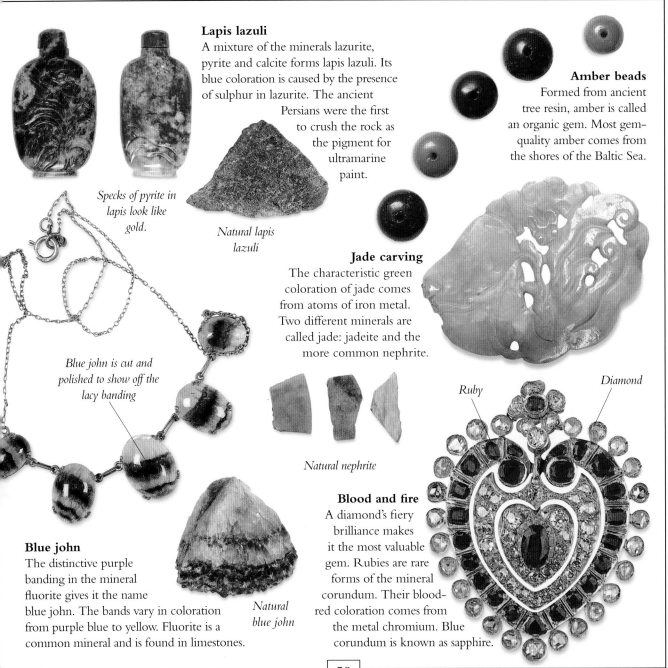

Lapis lazuli

A mixture of the minerals lazurite, pyrite and calcite forms lapis lazuli. Its blue coloration is caused by the presence of sulphur in lazurite. The ancient Persians were the first to crush the rock as the pigment for ultramarine paint.

Specks of pyrite in lapis look like gold.

Natural lapis lazuli

Amber beads

Formed from ancient tree resin, amber is called an organic gem. Most gem-quality amber comes from the shores of the Baltic Sea.

Jade carving

The characteristic green coloration of jade comes from atoms of iron metal. Two different minerals are called jade: jadeite and the more common nephrite.

Blue john is cut and polished to show off the lacy banding

Natural nephrite

Ruby

Diamond

Blue john

The distinctive purple banding in the mineral fluorite gives it the name blue john. The bands vary in coloration from purple blue to yellow. Fluorite is a common mineral and is found in limestones.

Natural blue john

Blood and fire

A diamond's fiery brilliance makes it the most valuable gem. Rubies are rare forms of the mineral corundum. Their blood-red coloration comes from the metal chromium. Blue corundum is known as sapphire.

USING ROCKS AND MINERALS

MANY of the materials around you are made from rocks and minerals. Ceramic mugs, tin cans and glass windows are just three examples. Many pigments, especially those used by artists, are made from particular minerals. You can make your own paints by crushing rocks in a mortar and pestle. Gold is one of the few metals that is found in its pure state in nature. It is sometimes found as nuggets in rivers. The nuggets can be separated from mud and gravel by panning and you can try this in the first project below. In the second project, with adult supervision you can experiment with one of the most widely used mineral materials – concrete.

Make paint
Using a mortar and pestle, crush charcoal, brown clay or chalk. Add a little cooking oil to make paint.

MATERIALS

You will need: gloves, trowel, soil, old wok, water, measuring jug, nuts and bolts preferably made of brass, deep tray.

Panning for gold

1 Put on gloves and fill a trowel with soil. Place the soil in an old wok, or shallow pan, along with about a litre (one quart) of water and some small brass nuts and bolts.

2 Swirl the wok around gently, letting the soil and water spill over the edge. Panning for real gold gets rid of the mud and water, leaving any large stones and gold nuggets behind.

3 When nearly all the water is gone, examine what is left. You should see that the nuts and bolts have been left behind, because they are heavier than the particles of soil.

Mixing your own concrete

1 Place one cupful of sand into a bucket. Then add two cupfuls of cement and a handful of gravel.

2 Add water to the mixture, stirring all the time, until the mixture has the consistency of oatmeal.

3 Pour the wet concrete on to a tray and spread out. Leave to solidify for about half an hour.

M A T E R I A L S

You will need: gloves, measuring cup, sand, bucket, cement, gravel, water, stirring stick, old tray, small thin box, foil.

Hand prints

6 How strong is the concrete block once it has set? Test its strength by trying to bend it. Can you rest a heavy weight on the block?

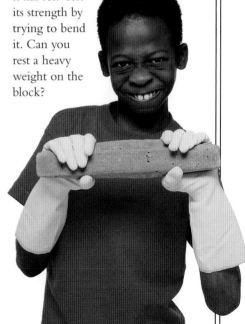

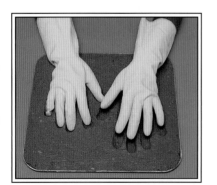

4 At this stage you can pattern the concrete. Make impressions of your hands (wash them soon after), or write with a stick. The marks will be permanent once the concrete sets.

5 You could make a solid concrete block like those used in the construction industry. First, line a small box with kitchen foil. Pour in the concrete and smooth the top.

ROCKS IN SPACE

Chondrite (stony) meteorite consisting mainly of the minerals olivine and pyroxene.

Iron meteorite consisting of nickle-iron, which is strongly magnetic.

Shergottite
(stony) meteorite consisting of two different basalt rocks.

Meteorites
There are three main types of meteorite – stony, iron and stony-iron. Stony meteorites (the most common) are made of rock, while the other two contain nickel and iron.

I^T is not only on the Earth that we can find rocks and minerals. Much of the rocky material in orbit around the Sun was formed at the time of the creation of the Solar System, some 4,600 million years ago. Some fragments of this material exist as small rock particles called meteoroids. Every day, tonnes of this material hit the top of the Earth's atmosphere. Here friction causes it to heat up and vaporize, sometimes causing a spectacular phenomenon called a meteor, or shooting star. Larger particles do not vaporize completely and a few actually hit the ground. These rocks are called meteorites. Some meteorites are from the Moon or Mars. They were chunks of rock that were thrown off the planet when rock fragments from Space bombarded the surface, forming craters. The surface of the Moon is littered with craters. When meteorite craters do form on Earth, they are usually covered over or destroyed by geological processes, such as the formation of mountains, or erosion by the weather.

Meteor Crater
This hole in the ground in Arizona, USA, is a crater. It was formed by the impact of a meteorite that fell about 25,000 years ago. About six craters of this size exist on Earth – most craters are covered up, filled with water, or have eroded long ago.

The red planet

Mars is called the red planet because its surface is covered with red iron-oxide dust. It is the most Earth-like of the planets and may hold important clues for Earth's future climate. Four huge volcanoes and an enormous canyon scar its arid surface.

Rocks on Mars

The *Pathfinder* mission landed on Mars in July 1997. Aboard was a robot probe, called the *Sojourner Rover*, which studied rocks on the surface and sent back photographic images.

Asteroids

Many meteorites are thought to be broken fragments formed by the collisions between asteroids. Most asteroids, also called minor planets, orbit the Sun in a belt between Mars and Jupiter. Larger asteroids probably have a metallic core, surrounded by rock.

FACT BOX

• About 382kg (840lbs) of rock has been brought to Earth from the Moon. The most common type of rock on the Moon is basalt. It is the same as the basalt that occurs on Earth and formed from solidified lava from volcanoes.

• Only one person is ever known to have been hit by a meteorite. It happened in 1954, in Sylacauga, Alabama. The person was not hurt, because the meteorite had already bounced on the ground.

Shooting stars

Meteoroids hit the Earth's outer atmosphere while moving at high speed. As they pass through the air, they heat up and begin to glow yellow-white, appearing as a bright streak across the sky. This is called a meteor, or shooting star.

INDEX